Western Steam Farewell

Darren Page

Ian Allan
PUBLISHING

To my dear Dad, for teaching me to look backwards as well as forwards.
And for my sons, in the hope that they will too.

Left: Vale of Rheidol 2-6-2T No 7 *Owain Glyndwr* hitches a lift on its return trip from Swindon to Aberystwyth. The V of R engines operated the last all-steam service run by BR and during the 1970s and '80s bore the corporate plain-blue livery complete with large double-arrow motif. As part of a revamp of the service all the engines were repainted in earlier colour schemes, including lined Brunswick green for No 7. This photograph was taken at Shrewsbury in April 1961.

Front cover: 'Modified Hall' No 7918 *Rhose Wood Hall* puts on a show through Grimes Hill & Wythall station. The popularity of these engines saw the class survive until the last knockings of steam on the WR. The last examples disappeared late in 1965, including those engines that had found a home on the adjacent LMR, which were replaced (for a few months) by 'Black Fives'.

Back cover: Collett '14xx' 0-4-2 tank No 1409 takes on water before heading out with one of the many local and stopping services from Gloucester Central station in March 1961.

Title page: Rebuilt from Churchward heavy 2-6-2T No 5115 in 1939, '81xx' 2-6-2T No 8109 was the last survivor of the class, making it through to June 1965. Here it is seen south of Acocks Green, Birmingham, with a stopping train for Leamington Spa in July 1964.

First published 2004

ISBN 0 7110 2998 9

Published by Ian Allan Publishing

an imprint of Ian Allan Publishing Ltd, Hersham, Surrey KT12 4RG. Printed by Ian Allan Printing Ltd, Hersham, Surrey KT12 4RG.

Code: 0407/B2

Preface

One fine summer morning a young man sat watching a motionless float as he fished on the Birmingham–Stratford canal. The fish were not co-operating that day, and his attention soon strayed to the passing traffic on the nearby railway line.

The young man was John Walter Page, my father, and the date (though never given accurately) was some time in the late 1950s. The railway network was enjoying something of an Indian summer in terms of revenue, and that morning the scene before him was typically Western Region. Express workings flew past behind 'Hall' 4-6-0s, stopping trains rumbled along behind Prairies and the omnipresent 0-6-0 pannier tanks. It was a wonderful sight for any enthusiast and one that couldn't last much longer. That thought brought about a sudden change in my father's interests. The fishing rods were left in the shed, and his other hobby — photography — was put to use recording what he could of the railway scene before steam disappeared for good.

Although he travelled far enough to record the great engines of the 'Big Four', my father was Birmingham-born and -bred. Having grown up in Acocks Green, his early memories of steam were coloured by the nearby North Warwickshire line. Not surprisingly he was a GWR man at heart, and much of his time was spent recording what remained of Swindon's influence, from the mighty top-link express locomotive through to the humble auto-train. He even photographed the sad relics languishing in the back yard at Swindon's workshops.

Following Nationalisation Britain's railway network was still one of the busiest in the world. During the 1950s the system could boast some 2¾ million users per day, whilst freight services dealt with nearly a million tons of goods and provisions every weekday. Yet things had changed: World War 2 had seriously drained national reserves, and, as part of the price of peace, Britain was facing the loss of her Empire. The war had also forced massive advances in internal-combustion-engine technology that would soon have far-reaching effects on the viability of steam power.

By the 1960s the pace of economic and social change within British society was beginning to have a marked influence on the rail network. Just as the railways spelled the end for commercial canal traffic the development of the road system began to offer serious competition to rail freight services, whilst growing prosperity amongst the working classes saw a rise in popularity for the motor car. The effective increase in personal liberty and choice drove the last nail into many a branch-line coffin. Once the arteries of rural and metropolitan communities, many lines could no longer muster the traffic to pay their way. Official policy within the British Transport Commission even started to favour the fanciful notion that the helicopter would form a viable part in the quest for an integrated transport policy!

Railway motive power was also caught in the midst of change. British Rail engineers introduced a number of standard locomotive designs, but when 2-10-0 No 92220 *Evening Star* was turned out by Swindon Works in March 1960, she became the last new steam locomotive commissioned for BR. Modernisation plans had been underway for some time, and a great many diesel and electric locomotives had already entered into BR service before *Evening Star* left the works.

As the new decade dawned 'dieselisation' was far from complete: many of the engines in service were of non-standard types, and some were none too successful. However, the writing was on the wall. Steam engines always required a great deal of maintenance, and their postwar performances had suffered due to inferior coal supplies and leaner engine-shed schedules. Despite the predictions from many enthusiasts, only five short years were left for this form of motive power on the Western Region.

Even in the face of so much change and BR's preponderance towards LMS design thinking, the Regional railways still held a strong affinity with the past. Many of the earlier locomotive designs had been withdrawn, but lots of train movements were still headed by Regional engines. The fact that a great number remained within pre-Nationalisation boundaries helped to reinforce regional stereotyping too. This link with the past was at its strongest on the Western Region, where a family of 4-6-0 and Mogul tender engines plus a disproportionate number of tank engines presented a scene that was unmistakably GWR to the death.

Nationalisation had put something of a stranglehold on Regional locomotive design, but by the 1950s a degree of autonomy had been handed back to Swindon. What followed was the development of diesel motive power subtly different from that finding favour elsewhere. Diesel-electric traction had gained in popularity, but such engines were relatively heavy and complex. Swindon designers did away with the electric traction motors and utilised viscous couplings between the diesel engine and drive wheels. The results were light, powerful and distinctive units that rapidly replaced steam-hauled freight and passenger services.

The GWR had also made use of diesel railcars during the 1940s. These simple diesel-mechanical units were successful enough to survive into the 1960s and were being joined by diesel multiple-units that were dependable, capable of long-range operation and offered passengers a comfortable and clean means of transport.

Realising that time was short, my father got busy with his camera using a mix of Agfa and Kodak film, most of which he developed at home. The following material has been selected in an attempt to cover as diverse a range of engines and locations as possible, and it is pleasing to note that, despite the general neglect characteristic of steam power during the 1960s, many of the shots depict locomotives in glorious condition, still on top of their work on a busy and extensive network.

Darren Page
Rednal, Birmingham
January 2004

Above: The pioneer 'King', No 6000 *King George V*, in fine trim at the head of the 'Cambrian Coast Express' at Leamington Spa in October 1961. The 'King' class was Collett's response to Maunsell's *Lord Nelson*, which produced a tractive effort greater than that of a GWR 'Castle'. The 'King' design, whilst unmistakably GWR 4-6-0, departed from Swindon's tradition of standardisation and employed a host of specially designed and enlarged components, even employing the first manual windscreen-wiper (fitted to the driver's-side cab window) ever seen on a GWR locomotive.

Right: 'King' No 6027 *King Richard I* at Leamington in October 1961. From this angle the double chimney is less obvious, but the route-availability markers on the cab side and the locomotive's general condition point to top-link WR power.

Left: No 6019 *King Henry V* glints in the weak winter sunshine as it leaves Paddington in February 1962. The 'King' class marked the zenith of GWR express-passenger-engine design. Due to good balancing inherent in the four-cylinder layout, the axle loading weight was allowed to creep up from the accepted British limit of 20 tons to 22½ tons without risk of increased stressing to track and bridges, but this new axle weight effectively restricted the route availability of the class.

Below: No 6020 *King Henry IV* in repose at Leamington in October 1961. Even though these engines were very close to withdrawal, they were always presented in a condition befitting their status.

Left: No 6000 *King George V* attracts admiring glances as it pauses at Wolverhampton Lower Level with the 'Cambrian Coast Express'. This engine was an enduring symbol of steam power and poise and put in 35 years' service for a total of nearly two million miles before it passed into preservation in December 1962.

Above: No 6017 *King Edward IV* departs Leamington at the head of a Wolverhampton–Paddington express in September 1961. Having reigned supreme on express workings since the late 1920s, the 'Kings' were withdrawn in quick succession as diesel-hydraulic motive power took the WR by storm.

10

Left: 'King' No 6021 *King Richard II* on 'Cambrian Coast' duty at Leamington Spa. These engines never suffered relegation from their intended express duties and remained a tribute to the hard work of the shedmen at Old Oak Common.

Above: No 6026 *King John* shows off its driving wheels and nameplate in this side-on shot at Reading in August 1962. Still spick and span, this engine was withdrawn just a month later and scrapped at Swindon Works.

Above: No 1019 *County of Merioneth* heads the northbound 'Pines Express' through Acocks Green, Birmingham, in October 1962. This famous service was re-routed in 1962 following closure of the Somerset & Dorset line and thereafter made its way to Birmingham through Oxford rather than over the Midland route through Gloucester.

Right: Just two months before its withdrawal, 'County' No 1010 *County of Caernarvon* was still exceedingly photogenic, being caught here at another famous spot for railway photography — Swindon running shed — on 19 May 1964.

Above: By 1964 many WR steam locomotives had disappeared and many more were lying fallow in quiet corners. One such example was No 1020 *County of Monmouth.* Photographed at Swindon in May, it had already yielded its name and numberplates, along with part of its running gear.

Right: The first of Hawksworth's ultimate two-cylinder 4-6-0s, No 1000 *County of Middlesex* stands proudly next to an English Electric Type 3 Co-Co diesel at Swindon. The 'County' class never achieved the level of acclaim bestowed on earlier 'Saints' and 'Halls'; only 30 were produced, and they gained a reputation for indifferent steaming, although this trait was improved when their boiler pressure was reduced.

Above: The WR adopted dieselisation as part of BR's modernisation plans and then promptly returned to ploughing its own furrow! Whilst diesel-electric motive power was gaining popularity on other Regions, Swindon was developing a range of powerful yet lightweight diesel-hydraulic locomotives. This photograph shows Swindon-built 'Warship' No D803 *Albion* charging north towards Dawlish Warren with a train for Exeter St Davids. The leading carriage is a Royal Mail car fitted with collection and drop-off arms that allowed the distribution of mail without the need to stop at secondary stations.

Right: Snow Hill station, Birmingham, is the setting for one of three eight-car diesel-electric units built by Metropolitan-Cammell for the Birmingham, Bristol and South Wales Pullman services. Designed for sumptuous and rapid transport, they were withdrawn first from the Birmingham service, following electrification of the West Coast main line. The two remaining services finished in May 1973.

Left: 'Castle' No 5085 *Evesham Abbey* looks fresh (if a little short of numberplates) as it runs light through Reading in August 1962. This engine started life in 1922 as one of Churchward's 'Stars', numbered 4065, and was rebuilt at Swindon in 1939.

Below: 'Castle' No 5098 *Clifford Castle* prepares for duty outside Shrewsbury shed on a freezing January morning in 1962. The engine clearly displays a Newton Abbot shedplate on its smokebox.

Above: Constructed in June 1937, 'Castle' No 5063 *Thornbury Castle* ran for just one month before being renamed *Earl Baldwin*. The 'Earl' names had been destined for the 4-4-0 '32xx' class being rebuilt from 'Bulldog' frames and 'Duke'-type boilers, but only 12 'Dukedogs' were named before the series was transferred to the 'Castles'. No 5063 is seen approaching Knowle & Dorridge in July 1964.

Right: 'Castle' No 5076 at Leamington in September 1961. Originally named *Drysllwyn Castle*, it was renamed *Gladiator* after the GWR decided to name 12 of its 'Castles' after aircraft used in the Battle of Britain.

Left: Constructed in 1937, 'Castle' No 5067 *St Fagans Castle* was allocated to Reading. By the time this photograph was taken at Leamington in October 1961 it had not been fitted with the double blastpipe and chimney; it had, however, lost its Collett-designed tender and been paired with one of the later Hawksworth type.

Above: One of the earliest 'Castles', No 4079 *Pendennis Castle* took part in the locomotive trials of 1925, running against LNER Gresley 'A1' Pacifics between King's Cross and Doncaster, where the Churchward design's reputation for fast, efficient running was confirmed. This photograph shows the engine at Tyseley with a relaxed crew just a month before withdrawal, preservation and eventual exile in Australia. Happily it has now returned to the UK.

Above: 'Castle' 4-6-0 No 7011 *Banbury Castle* participates in a pleasing scene as it reverses through Oxford station. *Banbury Castle* was one of the few Hawksworth 'Castles' not to receive a double blastpipe and chimney.

Right: No 5097 *Sarum Castle* prepares to take on water at Gloucester Central a few months after fitting of a new super-heater and double chimney. The 'Castle' was the most versatile WR express locomotive — light enough to range over virtually the whole system and strong enough for just about any duty.

Above: 'Castle' No 7002 *Devizes Castle* was treated to a new four-row superheater and double chimney late in life. It was photographed at Worcester Shrub Hill in May 1964, two months after its withdrawal; shortly afterwards it was acquired for scrapping by Cashmore's of Great Bridge.

Right: 'Castle' No 5089 *Westminster Abbey* seen in the last year of its life (1964) on a southbound parcels train at Acocks Green. The dire state of its exhaust emissions was not typical of GWR locomotives, even after suffering the effects of neglect and reduced coal quality. What was happening on the footplate at the time can only be guessed at.

Above: 'Hall' No 6927 *Lilford Hall* approaches Acocks Green, Birmingham, bound for Paddington with a mixed rake of maroon-liveried coaches.

Right: Even though 1960s steam working was characterised by neglect and decay, the occasional appearance of engines in ex-works condition could awaken memories of former glories. Here a pristine No 5964 *Wolseley Hall* heads an express at Stroud in March 1961.

Above: 'Modified Hall' No 6988 *Swithland Hall* attacks Hatton Bank with a mixed freight train in June 1964. Dieselisation had already taken a big chunk out of 'Hall' workings, and the successful introduction of Beyer Peacock 'Hymek' diesel-hydraulics on fitted freight trains really started to erode their position on the WR.

Right: 'Modified Hall' No 6989 *Wightwick Hall* arrives at Worcester Shrub Hill in October 1961. Withdrawn in June 1964 and acquired by Woodham's of Barry, this locomotive would become the 88th engine to depart Woodham's yard for preservation, in 1978 after purchase by the Buckinghamshire Railway Centre.

31

Below: No 5968 *Cory Hall* runs backwards around the sharp curve into Shrewsbury station during April 1961, affording a nice view of its Collett six-wheel tender.

Right: 'Hall' No 6948 *Holbrooke Hall* in ex-works condition at Worcester Shrub Hill in October 1961. Some 20 years after wartime operating conditions demanded that locomotive loading restrictions be exceeded, an additional 'X' symbol could still be found adjacent to the cab-side route and power-class markers on 'Halls', indicating that the practice was acceptable.

Left: No 5934 *Kneller Hall* emerges from the canopy at Birmingham Snow Hill station with an express freight. This undated photograph shows the gradually worsening condition of this station's platform canopies in the early 1960s.

Below: At the head of a rake of SR green coaching stock, 'Modified Hall' No 6967 *Willesley Hall* refills its tender at Goring troughs. The locomotive was not withdrawn until 18 months after this photograph was taken, surviving until December 1965 as one of the very last 'Halls' in service.

Left: 'Modified Hall' No 7908 *Henshall Hall* photographed from an unusual angle at Grange Road, Solihull — just south of Olton station — with a semi-fast passenger service in 1964. The 'Halls' were truly ubiquitous locomotives and roamed the entire Western Region, providing capable service in a variety of roles.

Above: 'Modified Hall' No 6964 *Thornbridge Hall* runs light from the shed for a turn on the 'Cambrian Coast Express' at Shrewsbury in January 1962.

Left: A 1933-built 'Hall', No 5936 *Oakley Hall* brightens a cold winter morning in Solihull with a ballast train. This engine remained in service until the final year of Western steam, not being withdrawn until January 1965.

Above: 'Modified Hall' No 6997 *Bryn-Ivor Hall* stretches its '5MT' power rating with an express freight running up through Wilmcote station just four months before withdrawal in November 1964. The steam from an assisting engine can just be seen at the rear of the train.

Above: Bound for Birmingham Snow Hill, No 6851 *Hurst Grange* passes Grange Road, Solihull, in July 1964. In common with many of the WR's steam locomotives, *Hurst Grange* was outwardly in poor condition by the mid-1960s, but it nevertheless put in another 13 months' service before withdrawal from Tyseley shed and was obviously still up to the rigours of express passenger haulage.

Right: 'Grange' No 6810 *Blakemere Grange* ambles through Willenhall Bilston Street with a mixed goods in August 1964. This class of engine was designed by Collett for intermediate passenger work. If plans had not been shelved because of World War 2 these engines would have taken over much of the work done by the Churchward Moguls. No 6810 was a Welsh engine, being allocated first to Cardiff Canton and later to Llanelli. It was withdrawn in October 1964 and scrapped by Bird's of Bridgend.

No 6858 *Woolston Grange* rests in the roundhouse at Tyseley shed in March 1962, next to a BR 350hp 0-6-0 diesel shunter. *Woolston Grange* was constructed in 1937 and spent much of its life allocated to Tyseley. The class was a very useful mixed traffic design, and, like many of its peers, this example remained in service until the end of steam on the WR.

In fine condition, 'Grange' No 6853 *Morehampton Grange* awaits
permission to leave Leamington Spa in June 1962.

Left: No 7808 *Cookham Manor* about to be uncoupled at Swindon following arrival with an SLS special in June 1964. Following withdrawal in 1965 the engine was bought privately and moved to Ashchurch for renovation.

Below: No 7807 *Compton Manor* photographed passing the tower as it leaves Shrewsbury station in April 1961. The complicated junction arrangement and signalbox are clearly visible in the background.

Left: No 7817 *Garsington Manor* reverses through Wolverhampton Low Level station in April 1961. Now into its 23rd year of service, the engine looked a little weather-beaten and was apparently suffering some problems with its reversing gear. The freshly applied warning stickers on the boiler sides and firebox attest to an added danger for engine crew, namely that of electrocution from overhead power lines.

Below: Churchward '47xx' 2-8-0 No 4707 photographed outside Tyseley shed in early December 1962. These locomotives represented the ultimate development by the GWR for heavy freight work, but they were also capable performers on express passenger services. Their first line of duty was night freight work, so they were not frequently photographed, but during the summer months they were often to be found rushing to the seaside with weekend holiday specials.

Collett '28xx' 2-8-0 No 3820 saunters through Cashes Green Halt with an empty mineral train in April 1963. This engine spent some time after the war renumbered as 4856 following conversion to oil-burning. Such experiments lasted a few years, but oil never proved a viable alternative to coal, and the engines involved gained a reputation for dirty working conditions on the footplate.

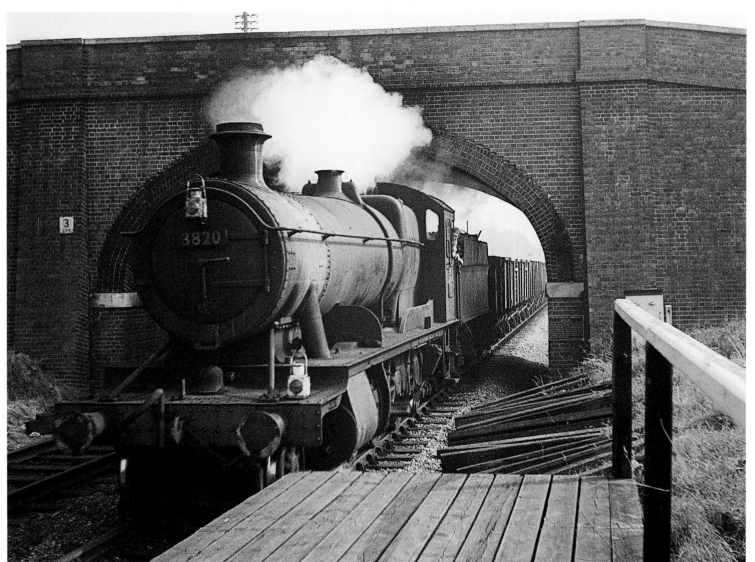

A smart example of Churchward's '28xx' class, No 2874 passes through Stroud in March 1961 and catches the eye of two young trainspotters who have gained access to the footplate of the '5101' Prairie standing at the adjacent platform.

Churchward '43xx' 2-6-0 No 7318 trundles through Gloucester Central with a mixed freight working in 1961. The Mogul wheel arrangement was adopted by the GWR following a trip by one of Churchward's engineers to the USA, where the 2-6-0 was widely utilised. The engineer involved — Harold Holcroft — was able to table a design for the GWR's own Mogul very quickly by adapting existing plans for a 2-6-0 tank locomotive. No prototype was produced ahead of the design's receiving official sanction because it was based on a host of standard Swindon parts.

A Churchward-designed '43xx' marshals a line of new cars from the Austin Plant in sidings at Knowle & Dorridge. The Churchward Mogul was perhaps not the prettiest of engines but was nevertheless a competent one and performed mixed-traffic duties across the WR in large numbers until the end of steam working. No 6364 was withdrawn in November 1964 — seven months after this photograph was taken — having been in service since May 1925.

Below: Collett '2251' 0-6-0 No 2211 runs tender-first through Wilmcote station as it assists No 4966 *Shakenhurst Hall* with a mixed freight in May 1961.

Right: Collett '2251' No 2276 waits to leave Shrewsbury General with an express for Mid Wales. Formerly based at Old Oak Common, this engine had moved to Machynlleth as older engines such as the 'Dukedogs' were withdrawn from the ex-Cambrian lines. At the time this photograph was taken in 1961 No 2276 was destined to give just one more year of service.

Left: Collett '2251' No 2253 awaits its turn at Honeybourne in May 1964. Built in March 1930, this engine moved from Bristol St Philips Marsh to Reading and finally to Worcester, where it saw out its remaining years (until March 1965) hauling secondary passenger trains.

Right: Collett-designed '2251' No 3217 approaches Claverdon with a stopping train bound for Leamington Spa in September 1963.

Right: Later the same day, the same locomotive catches the early evening sun as it runs light from Claverdon station down towards Bearley.

Above: By then the sole surviving 'Dukedog' in service, No 9004 was photographed at Wellington (Shropshire) in April 1960. Constructed in the 1930s from withdrawn 'Duke of Cornwall' and 'Bulldog' engines, these antiquated locomotives were proof positive that Swindon engine designers didn't go looking for something new when current stock and standard components could provide what was needed. As usual, the results were very competent, and the '90xx' class enjoyed an extended run on the ex-Cambrian Railways system through North Wales until usurped in the 1950s by Collett-designed 'Manor' 4-6-0s and '2251' 0-6-0s. No 9017 survives in preservation on the Bluebell Railway in East Sussex and has recently been beautifully restored to working order.

Right: One of the most famous of all GWR engines, 4-4-0 'City' No 3440 *City of Truro* had retired from active service in 1931 to become an exhibit at the old York Railway Museum. In 1957 it made a welcome return to the main line, hauling special trains until 1961, when it retired to the Swindon collection. This undated photograph is at least easy to place, with the adjacent warehouse in shot, and depicts the engine on display at one of the terminal platforms at Birmingham Moor Street station.

Left: One of the early, Swindon-built Western Type 4 C-C diesel-hydraulics passes the sandstone cliffs at Dawlish in the mid-1960s. The 'Western' class represented the final development of the large diesel-hydraulic on the WR.

Right: 'Western' Type 4 C-C No D1040 *Western Queen* following a low-speed collision with the rear of a car-transporter train at Knowle & Dorridge on 15 August 1963. The locomotive had its leading cab completely crushed but nevertheless was successfully rebuilt and continued in service until February 1976, by which time it had covered nearly 1¼ million miles.

Left: '72xx' No 7216 approaches Stroud station with a mineral train in March 1961. Although first envisaged by Churchward, the 2-8-2 wheel configuration was not tried until Collett rebuilt a Churchward 2-8-0 '42xx' tank made redundant by a decline in Welsh coal traffic. The results were enough to impress the GWR Operating Department, and sanction was given to modify more of the existing 2-8-0s, thereby increasing their coal and water capacity.

Above: '72xx' 2-8-2T No 7208 seen at Gloucester's Engine Shed Junction in February 1962 at the head of an express freight of fresh produce. Despite the success of Collett's redesign of the '42xx' 2-8-0T, the '72xx' class was sensitive to sharp curves by virtue of its long wheelbase. Following a number of derailments, certain sidings were placed out of bounds, and the class was also known to suffer water leaks from its tanks, due to flexing stresses.

Left: Churchward-designed '5205' 2-8-0 tank No 5258 with a ballast train at Gloucester Central. Collett had already proven the success of the 2-8-2T design following conversion of redundant '42xx' 2-8-0s, and a series of these rebuilds had been completed by the time No 5258 was constructed as a 2-8-0, along with 14 other examples, in 1940.

Above: Exemplifying the 2-6-2 wheel arrangement much favoured by the GWR for mixed-traffic work, 'Large Prairie' tank No 8104 receives attention to its left cylinder outside Worcester shed in May 1964. The '81xx' class were Collett rebuilds of Churchward's '31xx' (later '5100') class of 1903-6 and utilised higher boiler pressures and slightly smaller driving wheels than their donor engines to aid acceleration on suburban passenger work.
No 8104 was the last-but-one to remain in service, surviving until December 1964.

Above: '61xx' Prairie No 6112 backs down onto a stopping freight at Oxford station in June 1964. These locomotives began life on London suburban workings but started to roam in the late 1950s as their original duties were handed over to diesel multiple-units.

Right: '5101' 2-6-2T No 4144 in ex-works condition outside Swindon Works in May 1964. Just 13 months later this engine was consigned to Woodham's of Barry. Happily it was rescued by the Great Western Society in 1974.

'5101' No 4151 runs bunker-first into Bearley station in June 1964. Light passenger work had formed the mainstay of Prairie-tank operations all over the WR, but in the later days of steam the large-wheel types were to be found covering a wide variety of duties from express workings to banking and piloting activities.

'5101' 2-6-2T No 4176 shunts empty mineral wagons at Hatton
station on an icy day in early March 1963.

Left: '4575' 2-6-2T No 4588 runs light into Plymouth station in April 1962. This engine was withdrawn shortly after the photograph was taken and was acquired by Woodham's of Barry. Acquired by the Dart Valley Railway in 1970, it was subsequently restored to working order at BREL Swindon Works.

Right: '56xx' 0-6-2 tank No 6609 approaches Bentley Heath Crossing with an empty mineral train in October 1962. Like most of this class, No 6609 started its working life in Wales before moving to Tyseley. The 0-6-2T arrangement found favour with several Welsh railway companies prior to their incorporation with the GWR, and Collett obviously saw no reason to do anything different when supplying them with more modern engines. It was reported that a '56xx' ran better in reverse, utilising the trailing axle as a leading bogie. The entire class survived into the 1960s, and several examples made it into preservation following acquisition by Woodham's of Barry.

Above: Although the 0-6-0 pannier tanks were originally designed for shunting duties, a number of the principal classes were vacuum-fitted for passenger work. Here No 9471 of the '94xx' class reverses into Cashes Green Halt on its journey to Gloucester.

Right: Two '94xx' panniers, Nos 8400 and 9430, labour away at the tail of a freight train climbing the Lickey Incline in September 1963. The leisurely pace imposed on traffic as it ran up the 1-in-37 gradient of the old Midland line afforded engine crews and guards plenty of time to pose for photographs.

Above: '74xx' 0-6-0PT No 7418 runs past Blowers Green Junction and towards Tipton Fiveways with a single coach full of schoolchildren in June 1964. The '74xx' was similar to the Collett '64xx' in all respects but for the exclusion of motor gear for push-pull working.

Right: Collett-designed '64xx' 0-6-0PT No 6421 at Wellington (Salop) in October 1961. These engines were motor-fitted and designed for passenger work; as such, they were withdrawn from 1958 as dieselisation took hold.

Above: Twelve years on from nationalisation, '57xx' 0-6-0PT No 9621 stands adjacent to the coaling plant at Wellington, with GWR livery still clearly discernible under the grime.

Right: '57xx' 0-6-0PT No 8743 takes on water at Stroud station in March 1961. By this time considerable inroads had been made into what had been the most numerous class of engine in Britain; diesel railcars and multiple-units were being successfully used on suburban and cross-country passenger duties, whilst 0-6-0 diesel-mechanical shunters were proving very capable with their other principal line of work in the marshalling yards.

Above: The Great Western Railway pioneered the use of diesel railcars. This example is one of the 'razor edge' design from Swindon, built in 1940 with two AEC diesel engines together developing 210bhp. This photograph was taken at the Swindon Works 'dump' in May 1964.

Right: A single-car unit built by Gloucester RC&W Co photographed at Birmingham Snow Hill prior to a trip to Dudley in January 1959. Units such as this were typical of the motive power being used to replace steam-hauled auto-trains.

Collett '14xx' No 1472 at Sharpness station in May 1964. Steam-powered push-pull services were enjoying an Indian summer by this time, but, despite the progress made in diesel introduction, some GWR practice lingered on. Here the engine carries its headlamp on the buffer-beam rather than over the smokebox.

No 5815 was the last survivor from a class of 20 0-4-2 branch-line tank engines designed by Collett. Constructed in 1932/3, the '58xx' class were of a similar design to the more numerous '14xx' (originally '48xx') type but were not motor-fitted for push-pull work. This photograph was taken at Swindon Works dump in May 1964, three years after the engine was withdrawn.

Index of Locations

An example of the axle-loading sign once common on small road bridges crossing GWR tracks. These signs quickly became a target for collectors of railway memorabilia and must surely now be extinct in their natural habitat.

Full details of Ian Allan Publishing
titles can be found on
www.ianallanpublishing.com
or by writing for a free copy of our latest catalogue to:
Marketing Dept., Ian Allan Publishing,
Riverdene Business Park,
Molesey Road, Hersham KT12 4RG.

For an unrivalled range of aviation, military, transport and
maritime publications, visit our secure on-line bookshop at
www.ianallansuperstore.com

or visit the Ian Allan Bookshops in
Birmingham
47 Stephenson Street, B2 4DH; Tel: 0121 643 2496;
e-mail: bcc@ianallanpublishing.co.uk
Cardiff
31 Royal Arcade, CF10 1AE; Tel: 02920 390615;
e-mail: cardiff@ianallanpublishing.co.uk
London
45/46 Lower Marsh, Waterloo, SE1 7RG; Tel: 020 7401 2100;
e-mail: waterloo@ianallanpublishing.co.uk
Manchester
5 Piccadilly Station Approach, M1 2GH; Tel: 0161 237 9840;
e-mail: manchester@ianallanpublishing.co.uk
and (aviation and military titles only) at the
Aviation Experience,
Birmingham International Airport
3rd Floor, Main Terminal, B26 3QJ; Tel: 0121 781 0921
e-mail: bia@ianallanpublishing.co.uk

or through mail order by writing to:
Ian Allan Mail Order Dept.,
4 Watling Drive, Hinckley LE10 3EY.
Tel: 01455 254450.
Fax: 01455 233737.
e-mail: midlandbooks@compuserve.com

You are only a visit away from over 1,000
publishers worldwide.